*Mrs Na[...]
May [...]
Lord be with you always*

2019

Reflections From The Heart

By

Della Scott Thomas

Della Scott Thomas

Reflections From The Heart
Copyright © 2017 by Della Scott Thomas

All rights reserved, including the right of reproduction in whole or in part in any form.

No part of this publication may be stored in any retrieval system or transmitted in any form or by electronic, mechanical, photocopying, recording or otherwise without the written permission of the author, except the case of brief quotations embodied in critical articles and reviews.

Manufactured & printed in the
United States of America

ISBN-13: 978-1979017312
ISBN-10: 197901731X

Table of Contents

In Memory Of...

My parents, Pastor Johnie and Rosa Lee Scott, who instilled into our lives, the following spiritual values, 1)always represent Christ everywhere you go 2)love the Lord with all your heart, soul and mind, 3)give and it shall be given unto you, 4)be careful how you entertain strangers.

My older sister, Missionary Johnnie Scott Lamar Barnes, the oldest of 16 children, we called her Sister, was like a mother to all of us. I have fond memories of my sister as I sat at her feet as she combed my hair. She was a prayer warrior.

Geraldine Scott Gandy, who passed away at the age of 19 years old had 1 daughter, Virginia Mae, not even 2 years old at the time.

My sister Betty Scott Pittman, who was my best friend, died of the dreaded disease of breast cancer, leaving six children to grieve her demise, along with many family and friends.

Minister Shirley Scott Smith, a powerful woman of God.

My brother, born Burnell Scott, who became a prize fighter and changed his name to Prince Nakita Tarohocker.

My brother, Edward (Eddie) Scott, who entertained people for many years with his dance moves, also travelled and sang with the best of the best in the rock-n-roll field. Two years before his demise, he returned to his roots...Gospel and surrendered to Jesus Christ.

My grandson, Trevell, who was the apple of my eye, he had and always will have a special place in my heart. Before he was born, Trevell was chosen by God to be His messenger. He belonged to God more than to family. Every day I have to remember that he was here on this earth for only 22 years. Every day I also have to remember that God has him for eternity. I am grateful for the time God allowed Trevell Henry Brown, to bear fruit on this earth.

Acknowledgement

My brother, Pastor Robert and First Lady Michele Scott, thank you for the part you played in molding and shaping Trevell into the man that God purposed him to be.

My children, Glenda, Carolyn, Carlton, Treva and Ransford (Michael), thank you for the grandchildren you have given me and the great grands that followed. You are the sunshine that gives me joy, every day. "And we know that all things work together for good to them that love God, to them who are the called according to His purpose", Romans 8:28.

My grandchildren (great-grandchildren), Jonathan R. Brown (Destiny, Amari, La-neah), Corey T. Lee (Latehya, Kian, Donovan), Rhanada Green (Timaule, Timajay, Teraji, Jolvina, Joseph, Jr.), Taquanda S. Gibson (E'zariah, Eric, Emanuel), Chrisel D. Brown (Isaiah, Jeremiah, Elijah, Genesis), Dequiney Brown, Trevell H. Brown(deceased), Travis T. Brown, Timothy T. Brown, Darrin Mitchell, Kyron Mitchell, Timothy Lea, Barry Thompson, Jr. and godson, Donny Brown Jr., I love you.

My siblings, Rosa 'Pat" Scott Tucker, Elder Mary Scott Brown, and Martha M. Scott, thank you.

The Scott Family offspring, too many to mention by name and the 1st grand of the Scott Family offspring, Minister Dia Lamar Davis, thank you.

Sis. Cynthia Laramore and Sis. Verona Jacobs-Sams, thank you.

<u>Introduction</u>

I am an encourager. I worked at a radio station for six years as a gospel announcer in Garyville, LA. I used my time to show love and encouragement to others.

I began writing poems around the age of 10 years old for my sisters and brothers, for Christmas and Easter Programs.

Many years ago a well-known pastor passed away and I began writing sympathy words of encouragement for bereaved families. I could feel the hurt and pain that they were feeling.

God has given me the ability to reach the hearts of many with words of encouragement. Many of my writings were lost over the years. The Holy Spirit has always reminded me that the gift that was given to me must be shared with others, that they may bring encouragement to all who would read them. That is my prayer, that as you read my Reflections From The Heart, on the following pages, not only will you be encouraged, but that you will allow God to use you to be the encourager.

Our Family Prayer

Dear God keep our family safe
Help us to do Your will
Keep us with Your power and grace
Don't let us stray, please keep us near

We don't have everything we want
But God promised to supply our needs
Sometimes we complain about our don'ts
God Almighty is the greatest, indeed

Thank you Father for blessing our home
Protecting us from hurt and harm
Today you make our lives complete
I pray the Lord our soul to keep

<u>Ups and Downs of Life</u>

Each and every day of my life
I've tried to live from day to day
Sometimes I'm up, other times I am down
Within my heart, I know God is around

We all have our cross to bear
Press forward, if we want to meet Him there
When, How or Where
We're all in God's care

Some of my days were blue
I continue to hold my head high
Many days the sun would shine through
Late at night, I could always cry

Glenda, Carolyn, Carlton and Treva
God gave these babies to me
To watch over and keep them safe
Day by day, as I run this race

No Longer in My Life

The man I loved walked out on me
He tossed my heart into the red sea
He never looked back to see if I could swim
The hope of living seemed very dim

The man I loved no longer loved me
He left one day to be free
The strings were tied, but I must let go
The man I trusted isn't around anymore

The one I loved, he's gone for good
His tracks are washed away from the neighborhood
The grass is greener on the other side
In God's Word I shall abide

The Bible Brothers

Isaiah, Jeremiah and Elijah
Walking together side by side
Isaiah's favorite words, *it will be alright mom!!!*
Prophet Isaiah declares a message of hope

Jeremiah wants to know what's in it for me
Prophet Jeremiah declares that surrender to
God's will is the only way

Elijah, as strong and stubborn as a tree
Prophet Elijah prayed, realizing there's no
Limit to the power of prayer

Seek ye the Lord while He may be found
Call upon Him while He is near

A heartbroken prophet with a heartbreaking
Message of tears and compassion set apart
From the nation

How long halt you between two opinions?
If the Lord be God, follow Him, but if Baal then follow him

<u>Holding Hands with My Father</u>

My father used to walk and talk with me
Now, he is ill, and not what he used to be
The love for my father is real
He has touched my life for many years

In this life we've had ups and downs
Sooner or later he won't be around
Father will go to get his crown
Because of his share of ups and downs

When I was young, we worked in the field
Mom would prepare our favorite meal
I remember holding my father's hand
God has truly blessed this wonderful man

I'm remembering the good times we shared
Rain, sunshine, or stormy weather
My father will always be in my heart
When he parts this life, we'll never be apart

Heal Our Land, Lord

We are standing in the need of prayer
The light of Jesus shining everywhere
Can you hear His voice calling
Sinners around the world keep falling

Prayer is the key to Heaven eternal
Faith unlocks the door
Thank You Lord; Thank You Lord
Heal our land for evermore

Children are dying; crimes are rising
Crack cocaine is destroying lives
Death and destruction on every hand
Families are divided all over the land

We are standing Lord, we are standing
In the need of prayer
Lord Jesus, in our dying hour
We ask that You meet us there

We pray that our labor is not in vain
The saints of God lift up Your Name
We are standing Lord, in the need of prayer
Wrap Your arms around us
Let us know that You are there

My Father Knows the Way

My Father's way may not be your way
And your heart may ache with pain
Deep inside I know that you know He makes no mistake
Your hopes and dreams may fade away
But keep trusting my Lord to lead
Father God knows the way

There's so much you may not see
Your eyes are still so dim
But come while you can trust
And come while you can trust
And leave it all to Him

For by and by the mist will lift
And your darkness will turn to day
Lift your hands and praise His Name
For the One who led you all the way

A Father's Love

A Father's love grows deep inside
No matter how it appears to be
Many times his action can cause you to weep
But a Father's love will always keep

Sometimes family members seem uncaring
And there are days you feel all alone
Continue to hold on to your Father's love
It will keep you secure when he's gone

Remember the good things he does
And toss the bad into the red sea
Remember the times he gave you a hug
All the good memories will set you free

In My Father's House

In my Father's house, there're many mansions
They are prepared there for me
Flying high on eagle wings
I can sit at my Saviors feet
A prepared place for prepared people
In that home beyond the sky
There are many rooms in that mansion
Lord Jesus, do not pass me by
I know I have a seat in the kingdom
As I walk worthy of His calling
I will continue to do the Master's will
Your Grace and Mercy keep me from falling

Mother's Love is Always Near

Let me tell you about a dream
That I had the other night
The dream was so real
Her face shined bright as a light

When I woke the next morning
And looked all around
I was so very disappointed, I laid back down
I dreamed my mother was right here with me
We both were happy as we could be

I dreamed mother was cooking my favorite meal
When I came home from working in the field
Mother is no longer here any more
God took her home a few days ago
Oh what a dream, what a dream
I had the other night

A Mother's Love

A mother loves her children, day and night
Her love reaches far, when they're not in sight
Mother's love is deeper and wider than any sea,
There's no charge her love is free

She has been there in time of trouble,
Standing by her children, like no other
Her love is like a doctor when her children are ill
Her love is a towel when there's a spill

A mother's love is like a detective,
When her children are lost
Her love pays the salary, when there's no cost

A Mother loves her children both day and night;
She holds them in her arms real tight
A mother's love is always there whether
her children are wrong or right

<u>I'm Going Home</u>

I'm going home to a better place
I'm going home to see His face
I'm going home to get my reward
I'm going home, just to live with God

I'm going home to a place where there is no sorrow
Only peace, joy, and happiness for tomorrow
I'm going home to fly away
I'm looking forward to a better day

I'm going home where there is joy and peace
Trouble in the world will cease
I'm going home to wear a crown
Only then, will I lay my burden down

I'm going where the light shines so bright
I'm going home for evermore;
Everything will be alright;

I'm going home to take my rest.
Through hard trials and tribulations,
I've stood the test

<u>Look Up My Child</u>

As I look back over my life
Many obstacles in my way
I prayed many times
God brighten my days

Lord, You know I've struggled from time to time;
I've fallen by the wayside;
But God, in His wisdom said,
Look up my child; I'm always by your side

Each day I die to my flesh,
As I ask forgiveness for my sins
He washed me in His blood,
And gave me peace within

I looked over the mountaintop,
From whence cometh my help
I follow in His will;
That's when God orders my steps

God's Garden

Lord, You commissioned us to attend Your garden
However, there are obstacles in our way
We're standing in the midst of the garden
Facing confusion every day

There are many gardeners standing with us
Lifting our hands in praise
Committed to keep watch over Your garden
As we all run this Christian race

As leaders of Macedonia, we are planted along
The river bank, bearing much fruit in our season
Our leaves will never wither, all we do shall prosper
If we remember Who is the Gate Keeper over the garden

The trees You planted in the garden
Were all standing side by side
Once fertilized by the Holy Spirit
God's Word will then abide

There are many trees in this garden
North, South, East and West
As You commission Your saints to attend Your garden
We commit this day to do our very best

Walking in Spiritual Blessing

Doors open in our lives each and every day
As we walk according to God's will and way…
All things work together for our good
When we love the Lord, as we should

Nothing happens by coincidence
Because the plans of our lives are already laid out
God chooses according to His plans
He knew us before our feet ever touch this land

As we stroll down memory lane
Walking in Spiritual Blessing
How grateful we are for salvation
That covers our past, brings peace to our present
And assurance for our future

Doors open, doors close, how wonderful it is
To know the doors God is opening for Spiritual Blessing
Verses the doors He closes, that lead to destruction
Walking in Spiritual Blessings, through the open doors

Trusting the Word of God

We all gather for revival meeting
Praying that the Word of God
Would bring hope and freedom
Sinners sat on the mourner's bench
Surrounded by prayers from all the saints

The Word of God penetrating our heart
We listen and believe from the start
Prayer can change the hearts of men
If we open up and receive Him in

The bell was ringing; the choir was singing
While the train blew its horn
An old woman walked in, leaning on a cane
The preacher welcomed her with open arms

The revival meeting brought hope and freedom
For all the believers on the mourner's bench
Prayer and the Word changed hearts
Once we believed from the very start

Moment by Moment

It only takes a moment
To chase the blues away
It only takes a moment
To brighten the darkest day

It only takes a moment
To soothe the deepest pain
It only takes a moment
To come in out of the rain

It only takes a moment
For us to share our love
It only takes a moment
For us to give a hug

It only takes a moment
To lift a bowed down head
It only takes a moment
To get the lonely out of bed

Remember, it only takes a moment
For us to share our love
Looking unto Jesus, our Savior and Lord
Then smiles of joy, come down from above

<u>*God Will Never Leave You Alone*</u>

If you feel that all hope is gone
And everything in your life has gone wrong
If you are lost and can't find your way
Don't blame God
He has never left you alone

When your only son is on drugs
Lying, stealing, cheating, and misusing people around the world
Don't give up; victory is on the way
God will never leave you alone

When you feel that no one cares
And there is trouble everywhere
You know down in your heart
God has been there from the start
Don't give up' God will never leave you alone

The road has been rough, and the going gets mighty tough
Family and friends have let you down
My God steps in right on time
Don't give up, victory is on the way
God will never leave you alone

Sending a Distress Signal

Oh Lord, where are you? I feel so all alone. I received some disturbing news. You have allowed my beloved grandson "Trevell" to be taken away. Late in the midnight hour when my pillow is wet with tears I grieve, my heart aches for the touch of my grandson. I know that a loss is hard, and only You and time can heal. Help me to have Hope…Hope is built on nothing less than Jesus' love and His righteousness.

You promised never to leave me and that You would always be there for me even in my darkest hour. When I am going thru, I know that it's You that's carrying me. My heart is broken, I know You can and will mend a broken heart.

Earth has no sorrow that Heaven cannot heal. Your strength is made perfect. I'm sending out a distress signal, _"HELP LORD, I NEED Thee"_. I also know that You give and You also take away. Blessed be the Name of the Lord.

You allow storms in our lives and I know they don't last forever. Weeping may endure for a night. However, I'm trusting and very thankful that joy cometh in the morning time.

A Distress Signal Answered
HELP IS ON THE WAY

I'll Carry You through Your Pain

I know you sometimes use suffering
To sandblast me
My voice will praise You
Because You watch over me
You're my everlasting Father
You filled me with Your love
You wrapped Your arms around me
And showered me from above
Open my heart Lord, and take away the pain
Let your Sun shine through the falling rain
Take my hands! Lord, please hold me close
As I kneel down in prayer
All my burdens You will share
When I'm sad and low in spirit
Help me continue to keep the faith
Knowing in my heart, You won this race
Today is a new beginning, I feel You carrying me
Tomorrow the Angels will sing
Sweet, Sweet, Victory

"You have made known to me the paths of life; you will find me with joy in your presence".   Acts 2:28

There's Blessing in a Storm

When we're walking through the storm
And we cannot find our way
Stop complaining my children
In the storm you don't have to stay
The enemy tries to overtake us
Remember Who's holding our hand
He opened the red sea
We walk across on dry land

Blessing in a Storm
Joseph's storm was the pit
His blessing was the palace
Hannah's storm was Peninnah
Her blessing was Samuel
Paul's storm was a thorn in his side
His blessing was God's grace

Blessing in a Strom
Ruth's storm was a famine
Her blessing was a family Redeemer
She gave birth to Obed
Obed became the father of Jesse
Jesse became the father of King David
King David the linage to Jesus

Blessing in a Storm, count them one by one
Blessing in a Storm, the victory has been won
Saints of God there are many, many blessing in our storms
Without storms in our lives we would not know the power of God
Today we declare the Storm is Over

Down Memory Lane

Forty years ago
We strolled down memory lane
Loving each other
Yet, causing much pain

When we look back over our lives
And wonder where the time has gone
As we look within ourselves
Knowing God can fix whatever went wrong

Things go wrong, as they sometimes do
The heart will remember to always be true
The road is rough and the going gets tough
All hope isn't gone; God is seated on the throne

God sees the ending
He knows what will be
When we walk in His will and way
He promises us a brighter day

Forty years in the wilderness
We've seen the Promised Land
God parted the Red Sea;
We walked across on dry land

Walking Side by Side

Walking hand in hand
In the cool breeze of the day
The reddish leaves on the trees
Wintertime is on the way

Walking together up the mountain
Supporting each other in love
The wind blowing through the trees
God is watching us from above

When we reach the top of the mountain
Knowing we're in God's care
Just in case we stumble and fall
Without a doubt, God is always there

We're now on the top of the mountain
Standing side by side;
Looking down upon the earth
We can see God's handiwork

Time Has Made a Change

Time, time, time has made a change
Only God, our Heavenly Father remains the same
Come unto Jesus; don't delay
In the Son there is a brighter day

Time, time, time has made a change
God said Nicodemus, you must be born again
How can a man be born when he is old
Baptized in His name, you'll come forth as pure gold

Time, time, Oh Lord, time has made a change
The Angels in Heaven have signed my name
Let's give thanks for all He has done
This Christian race we all must run

Time, time, Oh Lord, time has made a change
There are times in our lives we all feel pain
Just a gentle touch of the Master's hand
Draws us near to the Promised Land

Light in Darkness

You touched my heart a few weeks ago
A man I never knew existed before
You came into my life and my love is real

That makes me happy, for making such a deal
You make me smile
When there's nothing to smile about
Just the thought of your love erases any doubt

You light up my life
In the darkness of the night
The hills and mountains we can climb
No matter how far from sight
You mean so much to me, because I love you so
Your love has given me the greatest joy I know

You are such a part of my life
In all I say and do, it will take a life time
Just to show you that my love is true

<u>Flowers in the Spring Time</u>

Flowers grow in the Spring time
You can find them everywhere
They cannot live without the rain
Look around; you will see them there

It may seem very strange
Maybe hard to believe
If flowers feel pain
Who knows they may even heal

Flowers come in all colors
Some red, white and blue
You can choose some for your mother
But remember to keep some for you

Flowers have a lovely smell
They were put on earth by Thee
They're too special for you to sell
If you wish, you can pick them free

I'm Still Here

Counting down, one by one
All reaching for the same goal
Pressing each day of our lives
For a miracle to unfold
I am still here

Waiting to be heard sometimes in the valley
It's hard to say the words, *I am still here*
I looked forward to this day
The dark clouds of my life have rolled away

I am still here, *I am still here*
I know from whence I came
I've climbed the mountain top to get here
But I know who's holding my hand

I am still here standing, but I am not alone
My friends and loved ones standing with me
While I sang this song
By the Grace of God, *I am still here*

He's Always There

There were nights I could not go to sleep
To many things on my mind
I prayed the Lord my soul to keep
Jesus came to me in His own time
Don't worry my child, I am here by your side
Be faithful and keep still

When the light appears, the darkness will hide
As long as I stay in the Master's will
When I call on the Lord, He answers my prayer
Jesus, Jesus, Hallelujah to Your Name!
When I need Him, He's right there
Through the sunshine and the rain

Who Is God?

God is the Creator, Savior and Lord
He hung the moon and the stars
Also parted the red sea, brought light
Formed darkness in order that someday
We will all be free

God created man and gave His only Son
So that the body of Christ
Would come together as one
He created the world in seven days
So therefore, all of God's Children
Should lift their hands in praise

Adam knew Eve and she bore two sons
Their names are Cain and Abel
Yet their spirits did not agree
Cain slew his brother

God asks a question, where is Abel?
Cain replied, am I my brother's keeper?
Yes! We are, because the Bible tells us so

<u>A Man Blessed with Faith</u>

A man blessed with a measure of faith
Touched by His power and His grace
Pressing forward toward the mark
With God's help, he will finish his race

Man of Faith heard the Voice of Jesus
Calling him to rest, lay down my weary child
Lay down and place your head upon My breast

Many people witness his faithfulness
Because he is a child of the King
He had been elevated to his mansion on high
A prepared place beyond the sky

Man of Faith flying on eagle wings
He shall bear no more pain
Family and friends must say good-bye
God shall wipe all tears from their eyes

Bow Down Before the King

We give our lives as sacrifices of praise
Though we are told, we don't need a Savior
And there's no reason to sing
We bow down before the King
Your great love remains the same

How high, how wide is Your unfailing love?
As far as the east is from the west
You took our sins away;
Placed them in the Sea of Forgetfulness
We received our blessing, once we confess

There's power in the Blood of Jesus
We're looking forward to a new season
God said, "Let my people go"
In Christ Jesus we are washed whiter than snow

The Potter and Clay

God, you're more than enough for me
You delivered me from darkness
And set my soul free
You are great and greatly to be praise
I shall behold Him, face to face

On Jesus, the solid rock I stand
Holding on to the Master's hand
My hope is built on nothing outside of Jesus'
Blood and His Righteousness

My way may not be easy, He said it would not be
I can make it only, if I put my trust in Thee
You are the Potter; I am the clay
Mold and shape me day by day

Jesus said, I won't let you fall if you lean on Me
You are bought with a price
And Jesus' Blood has set you free

Don't Look Back

When we are going through the valley
And can't find our way out
Don't look back as Lot's wife did
Unfortunately, she had many doubts

God has given us a way of escape
However, we can't let go of the past
Looking back where we use to be
Unsure of things we cannot see

When we're going through the storm and rain
Burden down with heart aches and pain
Don't give up help, is on the way
We can walk around Heaven all day

I praise you, Oh Lord! And will not be ashamed
The Angels in Heaven, signed my name
I am determined to live my life without chains
To live is Christ and to die is gain

On the Way to the Promise Land

The Israelites had to make bricks without sand
God's gift to them was the Promised Land
On the way out they complained; no food to eat
Even though they had shoes on their feet

They worshiped idol gods made from silver and gold
The half, my friend, has never been told
They forgot where God had brought them from
In order to get to the Promise Land
There's a race that must be run

God supplies all their needs,
According to His riches in glory
The younger Israelites were left to tell the story
Through trials and tribulations…
They made it to the Promise Land
All other ground, was sinking sand

Who's On the Lord's Side

Thank you Lord, for being the Holy One
Wrapped in a robe of righteousness
Father, Holy Spirit and Son
The body of Christ we gather in Your Name
From worldly pleasure, we will refrain

For me and my house, we'll serve the Lord
Standing together in one accord
He is our strength from day to day
Without Him we would fall
Peace and sweet rest
As we kneel before Him and be blessed

Joy and sorrow, there's hope for tomorrow
We are lenders, not borrowers
Daily, walking close to Thee
Your face to face we shall see
Let it be, Dear Lord, let it be

Sowing and Reaping

We all must reap what we sow
The Blessing of God knocks on our door
If we believe that His Word is true
His precious promises will see us through

When we sow good seeds, we'll reap a great harvest
Always remember to fertilize it with love
God sends His rain and sunshine down from above

Sowing seeds of righteousness, we'll inherit eternal life
As we present ourselves, as a living sacrifice
Holy and Acceptable unto God

Lord, I yield to You my life
I will do what You want me to do
I rest in Your assurance that Heaven will be my home
Not because of what I've done, but because of You

*Be not deceived; God is not mocked: for whatsoever a man soweth that shall he
also reap. Galatians 6:7 KJV*

Show Me Your Way Lord

There are days I know I'm not in God's will
Resentment and anger try to creep in
Lord, I need your Mercy and Grace
Help me Father to continue the right way

Trials and tribulations are on my back
However, I know in my heart God is able
My God can and will turn things around
When I push myself away from the table

There are times when I can't find my way
I know the monthly bills are here to stay
Cover me Lord with Your blood
Fill me with Your Grace and Your Love

Lord Jesus, You didn't say the road would be easy
I've known this from the beginning of time
You promised to supply my needs, freely
I will forever keep You on my mind

Through the storm, the rain, heartache and pain
Daily, I call on your Holy and Righteous Name
Your forgiveness is not in vain
Thanks for being in control of all things

When the telephone rings, I'm not sure who's on the line
It sometimes stops me in my track
Lord God, I need a little more time
Help me to press forward and not look back

Although I give my offering sometimes
It doesn't seem that it's enough
Oh Lord, things are tough
However, my tithes must come off the top

I know this season will not last
Down in the Valley, this too shall pass
God will make a way, His promises are true
He is God Almighty, He can make things brand new

I'm standing on the threshold of faith
Trusting God to run this race
Climbing this mountain, one day at a time
Jesus' first miracle, was turning water into wine

<u>Testimony</u>

I've got a wonderful testimony
I thank God that I'm still alive
Each and every day; He'll always provide

Thanks for all You've done
From the rising, to the setting of the sun
From the day I was born
My God never left me alone

Even when the odds were against me
Love said, not so
I'm grateful for one more chance
In the spirit I will praise God and dance

On a stormy sea; Jesus, speaks to me
I surrender my body and soul
The best is yet to come
Now my work on earth is done

Welcome, my child, your race has been won

Cookie

I'd like to take this time to say
Just how I really feel
When we met it was a wonderful day
My love for you was truly real

You don't have to give birth to a child
To care for them so much
I thank God every day
For bringing you my way

If I would have placed an order
Not knowing what to expect
I accept you as a daughter
Cookie, there's no regrets

Happy Holiday, Air Mail

Take a Box, fill it with Hope
Seal it with Understanding
Wrap it with Joy and Peace
Take a ribbon and tie a knot of Happiness

Stamp it with Forgiveness
Take it to the Post Office
In the name of Love
Airmail it, Special Delivery, to Heaven above

Recipe for Friendship

4 cups of _understanding_
Mix it with _forgiveness_
Add a tablespoon of _laughter_
Blend in a cup of _peace_
Sprinkle a dash of _joy_
Bake it with _wisdom_
Top it with _kindness_
Serve it with _happiness_
Seal it with _compassion_
Mail it in the name of _love_
Receive it in _faith_

Fond Remembrance

Thinking very special
Of the thoughtfulness you've shown

Thinking of the joy you bring
To everyone you've known

Wishing words could say
How much it meant the whole year through
Just to know someone as wonderful and as special as you

Love Isn't Love Until You Give It Away

Some time it's hard to explain
The pain that surrounds our heart
Being afraid to let go
It would mean we'd have to make a new start

When you lay awake at night
Thinking about what used to be
Deep in your heart
You know God has set you free

Laying awake at night
With the memory deep inside
Oh, how we want to let go
But old memories keep knocking on the door

Love isn't love until you give it away
Share it with your enemies day by day

Thank You

One of Gods greatest blessings
Is His gift of special people
Who touch our lives with kindness

Thanks is such a little word
That means so very much
Words cannot express my gratitude

Thanks for attending my Birthday celebration
It was special because you were there
I pray God's Blessings upon you
As He keeps you in His care

Easter and Christmas Time

Christmas time is here again
I hope you all enjoy
The recitation we bring to you
From all these girls and boys
This is the time we come to assemble
For there is no better day
We thank Christ our Savior
For leading us the way

Easter time is here again
I hope you all enjoy
The recitation we bring to you
From all these girls and boys
This is the time we come to assemble
For there is no better day
We thank Christ our Savior
He rose on Easter Day

__Happy Anniversary__

Thank you for the years we shared
Thank you for the children we bared
You made my life so complete
When you swept me off my feet
I gave you my heart and the best of my love
God watched over us from Heaven above

Husbands and wives dwell together in Harmony

And the Lord make you to increase and abound in love one toward another and
toward all men. Even as we do toward you. 1Thess.3:12

God Cares

I can't take away the heartache
That lingers deep inside
I can't take away the sadness
That's always there in sight
I know who can dry your tears away
Our Heavenly Father listens when you pray

Running the Red Light of Life

Every light has an intersection
As we travel to our destination
Looking forward to journeys end
It's possible to encounter a Red light again
Waiting for the light to change
Then we're on our way
Remember caution comes before red
However in our lane we must stay
There's a split second between yellow and red
Don't be in a rush and run the light
Danger may be lurking ahead
An accident could be just insight
Running the red light of life
Taking a chance each and every day
Let the Holy Spirit be your guide
Jesus is Life, truth and the way

Greater love hath no man than this that a man lay down his life for his friends.
You are my friends if ye do whatsoever I command you
John 15:13 KJV

It's Already Done

Come as you are
The best is yet to come
There's no secret what God can do
What He did for others He'll do for you
Today is a new beginning
Once you leave your Past behind
Reaching for a higher goal
The Word of God will unfold
You tried it your way for oh so long
Never once did you pick up the phone
Every night, your mother shed many tears
The pain in her head is very real
The door is still waiting for you to walk through
Hanging on the hinges of love
God watches you from above
You know not the day, nor the hour
When the Son of Man will come
God has given you the power
The race for eternal life must be run

SPECIAL TRIBUTES

Great Is Thou Faithfulness

(Pastor & Lady Cynthia Harris)

Faithful to the call of Christ
We're honoring the man and woman of God
Touched by the power of grace
Pressing forward to run this race

Faithful to the call of Christ
Thru the storm and rain
They're casting their cares at His feet
Holding firm to the Master's Hand

Faithful to the call of Christ
Lord keep them in Your Will and Way
Standing on God's promise
They surely can face another day

Macedonia Missionary Baptist Church
We give honor where honor is due
To our Pastor and first Lady Harris
We extend our love to you

Birthday Greetings

(Pastor C. Regi Rodgers)

Meeting in the Throne room each and every day
Leading God's people all the way
Pastor Regi, a modern day Moses
Many are called, but few are chosen
We give honor where honor is due
Our love is extended, always unto you

Happy Birthday Pastor
We greet you in the Name of Jesus
Today is a good day, we know this is our season
We bless God for your faithfulness
As you minister to God's people each and every day
We thank God, Our Father, for bringing you our way

Friendship

(You Know Who You Are)

I thank God for our friendship
We've been friends for many years
Through the thick and thin
We've shared each other's laughter
From way back when
Friend girl, we call each other
Which represents our love
We're connected together in the spirit
God showers us from above
Thinking often of you
Even though we're miles apart
We're together in the spirit
Because I carry you in my heart

Women Waiting Upon The Lord
(Happy Birthday Michele Scott)

Hannah waited with expectation and hope. She prayed within her heart, her mouth moved, not a word was heard. She knew the misery of waiting for a dream that did not come true, yet she poured her heart out to God because she knew what He could do. Could it be that Hannah learned what we need to learn? It's not by strength that we prevail. We concentrate on our needs, instead of on God. The scripture says over and over again, wait, for the Lord, not for the things you want, wait, It says, on the Lord.

Ruth waited for her redeemer as she gleaned in the field preparing for the day she would receive her meal. Boaz took Ruth and she became his wife. God enabled her to conceive and she brought forth a child. Ruth made a commitment. She was determined in her heart to stand by Naomi and they would never be apart.

Esther was placed in the King's household by divine appointment. Through fasting and praying, she went before the king even though she knew it was against the Law. She responded to the call.

The woman with an issue of blood, waited with expectation, pushing her way through the crowd, yet she remained patient. As she reached to touch the hem of His garment, while kneeling in the streets, she knew she would be healed down at the Savior's feet.

Irene Robinson waited for her special day, December 2, 1960, God already prepared the way. Before the foundation of the world, before Irene knew Bill, *Michele had been chosen to do the Master's will*. She was the youngest of three siblings. She picked up a guitar and began to play. The first band, Gazelle, was now on the way. In 1990, she realized that she was being lead in a different direction. She waited for her Boaz. He who finds a wife, finds a good thing. In 1991, Michele met Robert Scott. The two were a match made in Heaven. In April 1992, they became one...one body, fitting, joined together. "For we are taught of God, to love one another." Michele and Robert stand firm on the foundation of unity, peace and harmony. "If we walk by Faith and not by sight, we are secure, we don't need to see it just to believe it." Now after you have prayed, still be silent, be quiet, but in that time of waiting, be filled with expectancy and hope.

"But they that wait upon the Lord shall renew their strength; they shall mount up with wings as eagles, they shall run and not be weary, they shall walk and not faint".

Humbly submitted by *Della Scott Thomas*

Woman of Courage

Magnify the Lord with me and let us exalt His Name together. I sought the Lord, and he heard me and delivered me from all my fears.

Psalms 34:3-4

Have been crucified with Christ and I no longer live, but Christ lives in me.

Galatians 2:20

Children, be glad for all God is planning for you. Be patient in trouble, and always be prayerful.

Romans 12:12

Humble yourselves under the mighty power of God, and in His good time, He will honor you. Give all your worries and cares to God for He cares about what happens to you.

1 Peter 5 : 6-7

Encourage those who are timid. Brothers and sisters we urge you; warn those who are lazy, take under care of those who are weak, be patient with everyone.
.

1Thessolonians 5:14

Lay not for yourselves treasures upon earth where moth and rust doth corrupt and where thieves break through and steal, but lay, yourselves, treasures in Heaven.

Matthew 6:19-20

Even strong young lions sometimes hunger; but those who trust in the Lord will never lack any good thing.

Psalms 34:10

So we praise God for the wonderful kindness He has poured out because we belong to His Dearly Loved Son.

Ephesians 1:6

Confess your faults one to another and pray one for another, that ye may be healed. The effectual fervent prayer of the righteous man availed much.

James 5:16

Obey your leaders and submit to them, for they are to keep watch over your soul.
.

Hebrew 13.17

They that wait upon the Lord shall renew their strength they shall mount up with wings as eagles; they shall walk and not faint.

Isaiah 40:31

Trust in the Lord with all your heart and lean not unto your own understanding.

Proverbs 3:5

<u>Woman of Faith</u>

A *Woman of Faith* walking in God's will and way
Striving to give him glory each and every day
To live is Christ and to die is gain
Walking through wilderness
God showers with rain
The path of the Just is as a shining light
Following God's instructions…morning, noon and night
Connie will not compromise
Pressing on to win the prize
In Christ Jesus she goes the distance
A *Woman of Faith*, like a tree planted by the rivers of water
Bringeth forth much fruit in her season
Without fail her leaves never wither
Whatsoever she doeth shall prosper
A *Woman of Faith*, her husband can trust her
She will greatly enrich his life
She is a capable wife and mother
Her son arises up and calls her blessed
She is energetic and strong
She is a *Woman of Faith*, touched by God's grace

Glenda, My Daughter
Presented to: My First-Born Child

Who is she?
My wonderful daughter

God gave you to me, fifty-seven years ago
You came into my life, such a joy…my first-born child

Glenda

A daughter, sister, wife, and mother
Very special indeed, like none other
I pray God's blessing upon your life
To go deeper depth and higher ground

Glenda

In God's presence comes what may
Today it brings strength and contentment to your life
As you travel along God's way
Love, peace, happiness

Mom

"This is He"
Pastor Robert L. Scott Sr.

Called to pastor-ship at this particular time
The prophetess heard the Word of the Lord
God had Pastor Scott on his mind
I'm calling you to watch over my sheep
Speak the Word, be humble and meek
When trials and tribulations come your way
Remember God in His wisdom, there is a brighter day
God parted the red sea, the Israelites walked across on dry land
Remember my son, I hold you and the world in My Hand
Hold on my child and don't let go
How did you get here?
Only God knows
I have written My Word upon the table of your heart
I have been with you from the very start
This is the day that the Lord has made
Rejoice and be glad

Then Samuel said to Jessie, "Are all your sons hear?" And he said, "There remains yet the youngest but behold, he is keeping the sheep". And Samuel said to Jessie, "send and get him, for we will not sit down till he comes here". And he sent and brought him in. Now he was ruddy and had beautiful eyes and was handsome and the Lord said, "Arise, anoint him, for this is he".
1 Sam 16: 11-12

Rosa Lee Scott, Rev. Johnie L. Scott, Missionary Johnnie Scott
Barnes, Trevell H. Brown, Missionary Shirley Scott Smith,
Edward H. Scott, Betty Scott Pittman, (Rosa Scott Tucker,
Prince Nakita Tarohocker...not pictured)

<u>*Gone, But Not Forgotten*</u>

Early in the morning, the dew was on the roses
My mother made preparation for her home in glory
She was on her way to a church meeting
Knowing in her heart, she would receive her greeting

The week before, her face was a glow
St. Peter's horn would soon blow
My mother was dressed, not to be late
The death angel was already waiting at the gate

Mother made her way to the alter
She asked forgiveness for all her faults
Mother sang a song and sat down
It was her last day on earth, she was Heaven bound

In Loving Memory of My Mother, Mrs. Rosa Lee Scott

The Angels and Me

The Angels kept watch by night in room 733
I won't let go until you bless me and set my dad free
The Angels surrounded the room, as they kept watch by night
I could see my daddy watching, behold there is the light

As morning light appeared in room 733
Behold a new day, that God had shown me the way
I walked over to the window, while looking through the pane
I knew _The Angels_ were waiting, because I began to hear them sing

I called upon the Lord, God heard my cry
He said, "Don't worry my child, _The Angels_ are standing by"
As I sat there waiting in room 733
Time was slipping away from my daddy and me
The bells were ringing, _The Angels_ were singing
Hallelujah, Sweet Victory

In Loving Memory of Rev. Johnnie L. Scott

There's Safety in the Master's Arms

There's safety in the Master's Arms
The final race has been run
Flying high on eagle's wings
Making this journey In Jesus' Name

There's safety in the Master's Arms
Through the Blood of Jesus, God's only Son
To live is Christ and to die is Gain
Warren's footprints washed away by the rain

There's safety in the Master's Arms
The Battle is fought, and the victory is won
Landing safely in a Home on High
A prepared place beyond the sky

There's Safety in the Master's Arms
The Race was won by Warren
Keep in mind, he's in God's Care
Oh what a Day of Joy it will be to get there

In Loving Memory of Warren Logan

<u>*Woman of Wisdom*</u>

Woman of Wisdom, standing strong and tall
Holding the Savior's Hand, he dare not let her fall
She laid aside every weight, through prayer and the Word of God
Even the same days, seemed very hard

She walked many years with the master by her side
Humbly at His Feet, the Holy Spirit as her guide
God knew the plans he had for her
To love the Lord thy God, like none other

Woman of Wisdom, touched by grace
Standing on His promises to run this Christian race
Trusting the Lord, each and every day
God ordered her footsteps along the way

Older and wiser, yet harmless as a dove
She has been here 107 years, filled with God's love
She stood the test of time with God forever on her mind
Sister Lillian Phillips, *Woman of Wisdom*
Sweetest woman in town

Tribute
Sister Lillian Phillips – 107 years old

In Loving Memory

Edward Henry Scott (Eddie)
Sunrise July 21, 1948 – Sunset October 4, 2013

Today is a good day, in all things give thanks
We give God praise for the ups and downs
Eddie knew one day he would receive his crown

Eddie may not have done everything right
And maybe he did all he could do
As he walked across this land
He extended his love unto you

"We walk by faith and not by sight", as we read the Word of God
"Eddie" fought a good fight
The seed of his body, the offspring of his life
He asked God's blessings to protect and provide

"Eddie" prayed that God would keep his family
In His loving care, in the twinkling of an eye
He will meet you all there
Gone but not forgotten

In Loving Memory

Ruth Alma Stephney Buggs
Sunrise November, 29, 1927 - Sunset December, 19, 2013

To Mother Buggs' Children

"Jessie"

Mother Ruth Buggs, a child of the King
She pressed forward many years in Jesus' Name
Gone but not forgotten, she will forever remain in your heart
When you feel sad and lonely, know that you are never apart

"Jennifer"

You're all in the Master's Hand – He knows what's best for you
He has brought you from a mighty long way
He will continue to see you through
Stand on the promises of God, He's watching from above
Filled with His goodness, wrapped in His love – "But God"

"William"

In my Father's House there are many mansions
Way beyond the sky, God has prepared a home for Mother Buggs
You will see her again in that great by and by
Keep the faith family
God will help you stay in the race

"Bruce"

Mother Buggs, a virtuous woman
Her price was far above rubies
Strength and honor were her clothing
She rejoiced as her children called her blessed
She taught them wisdom, kindness, and love
May the praise be, the family I've raised

"Barbara"

There's safety in the Master's Arm
The final race has been run, flying high on eagle's wings
Making the journey in Jesus' Name, to live is Christ, to die is gain
Mother Buggs' footprints have been washed away by the rain
Safe in the Master's Arm
Today there's no pain

In Loving Memory

Mrs. Mildred L. Roach
Sunset 1922 – Sundown 2010

A bright star in God's majestic crown
It's hard to understand when death comes our way
Sometime it's hard for us to face another day
But God in His wisdom, looking down from the sky
Will help us understand it better, by and by

Mother, Grandmother, and Friend
The one there for all she loved, until the very end
A bright star in God's majestic crown
The gleaming shine of the sun, which never goes down

Therefore, God decided to replant this rose
In a place where she'll never grow old
This beautiful rose will remain eternal in our hearts
To grow forever and never wither apart

Her earthly footprints, though washed away
Now stand before God as her soul gives praise

A Mother's Love

When God gave you your son, he was just a loan
How, when or where, God would someday
Call him home to a place beyond the sky
You will meet him again in that great bye and bye

A mother's love reaches higher than any mountain
Deeper than any sea, there's no charge
Mother's love is always free
You prayed for your son each and every day
For God to protect him, as he traveled the dangerous highway

Let not your heart be troubled
God blessed you to be a good Mother
You loved your son and you did your very best
He was presented unto the Father, He did the rest
Emanuel fought a good fight and ran his race

In order to see His Savior face to face
Precious in the sight of God is the death of his faithful one
A Mother's love shines bright as the sun

A Woman of Strength and Courage

A wife, first lady, mother, grandmother, great grandmother, sister
and friend;
The one's she treasured until the very end

She treated everyone with respect.
Their lives were changed and she had no regrets.
She loved her family and put them first, knowing
That her time was limited here on earth.

Family, friends and other let slow down enough
To consider what true love really is.
Sis Jessie's name would be at the top of the list.
Because she lived it in God's will.

She is gone but not forgotten, touching lives
In manyways, safe in the Master's arms,
She stands before God, and gives him praise.
Remember the good times you shared
Leave the pain and sorrow at the Master's feet.
Keep her love in your heart.
She'll be there in spirit and never part.

Pastor, it's time to say your goodbyes.
I know it's hard for you to understand.
Your help meet won't be around anymore.
God has planted this rose high upon the Heavenly shores.

In Loving Memory

Lula Belle Knight-Shell

Sister to sister, touching each other's heart,
Joined from birth to never be apart;
The death angel came in the mist of the morning;
To take your sister to her heavenly home.

Seize the moment to remember when;
And treasure the good times you shared back then.
A time to weep, and a time to laugh;
A time to mourn and a time to dance.

Now is the time to dance your sorrow away;
God's promised tomorrow will be a brighter day.
Brothers and sisters, you're in God's care;
One of these days, we'll all get there.

In a moment; in the twinkling of an eye;
We'll all see Jesus in that great by and by.
The Kingdom status is for each of you;
Just keep the faith and Jesus will see you through.

In Loving Memory

Pricilla Lee Brown
Sunrise Sept. 12,1961 – Sunset Oct. 7, 2013

Daughters, sisters, wife, mother and friend
Those she treasured until the very end
Remember the days when you heard laughter together
Rain sunshine or stormy weather

The joy of siblings watching out for each other
Sisters and brothers giving strength to one another
You prayed in the spirit to overcome obstacles
That was in your way, God in His wisdom and a
Mother's love brought faith a brighter day

Although your heart is heavy because of the pain
You feel inside. Family and friends you can make it
God is always standing by
Remember Pricilla's love never comes to an end

Gone but not forgotten.

In Loving Memory

Sister Bettye Murray
February 9, 2013

Today your heart is heavy
Because of the pain you feel inside.
Remember you can make it;
God is always standing by.

The pain you feel deep inside
Will not last forever;
I promise you can make it my child
God will leave you never.

God in his wisdom
Looking down from above
You can make it my child
I extend to you my love.

It matter not what you are going through
God will take care of you
Through the storm and the rain
God in heaven can do all things
In the mist of your sorrow you can make it.

To Marva Murray & Family
Humbly Submitted by Della Scott Thomas

In Loving Memory

Pastor Joseph Thomas

Pastor Thomas of St. Luke Baptist Church,
Leading the flock like none other,
Family and friends gather today,
To celebrate a home-going as he passed this way.

His footprints have been washed away,
From the face of time,
As pastor of St Luke Baptist Church
He will always be a friend of mine.

Today is the home-going for our pastor and friend,
Who fought a good fight, until his destined end.
The road was rough and the going got tough,
Our father looked down and said, "My son, that's enough."

Pastor Thomas kept the faith, as he endured the difficult race,
Knowing at the end, he would see Jesus face to face.
To live is Christ, and to die is gain,
Sooner or later, losing a loved one, others too will experience this
pain.

Reminiscence on the happy times we shared,

Jesus said, "The cross alone, is not yours to bear."

God graced Pastor Thomas, with many years on this Earth;

But he left a legacy for many that knew him, not limited to the church.

His voice was heard; by boys, girls, women, and men,

Today we share our love, with family members and friends.

This moment we sadly share our pain and sorrow;

But the promises of God, assures me, joy will come tomorrow.

Today, our hearts hang tremendously heavy,

Because of the sadness that has touched our lives,

The home-going of our pastor and dearest friend;

The treasured memory of his love shall always in my heart, abide.

In Loving Memory

Jayson, Steven & Vincent Warren
Touching Lives In Many Ways

There once were three little babies
Each born on different days
Touching their families lives
In many special ways.

Three babies became little boys
They went to school each day
Carrying their books and toys
Touching lives in many special ways.

Jesus Christ, knows the way
It's hard for us to understand
That he came to take them home that day
Touching lives in many special ways.

Jayson, Steven and Vincent Warren
Members of the hymns of joys
Jesus summons them home to stay
Touch our lives in many special ways.

Presented on Friday, December 20, 1996
Della Scott Thomas Gospel Production

To Pastor Raymond Thompson & Family

I Knew You Were There
When you were going through the storm and rain,
Many days you suffered heart ache and pain
I Was There

You did not know if you could face another day,
I gave you strength to continue in my way
I Was There

Your smile, your laugh, you even visited the store
You knew the Death Angel would soon knock on the door
I Was There

You said your goodbye in your own special way,
To leave your memory in their hearts to stay
I Was There

You fought a good fight my child; you kept the faith,
Early in the morning you won your race
You Knew I Would Be There

God Is Always Standing By

When you were blessed with a child it was only just a loan
How, when or where, God always call them home.
However, it doesn't lessen the pain that you feel deep inside.
Remember my friend, God is always standing by.

The lost you feel inside will remain there forever.
But God said in his word, "I will not leave you ever."
Although the tears will fall like rain drops from the sky.
But God in his wisdom is always standing by.

He said, "be aware my child I hold you in my hand."
I felt the hurt and pain as I walked across the land.
Now I will carry your pain, I'll wipe your tears away,
Hold firm to my word I promise; there be a brighter day.

<u>In Loving Memory</u>

Your father was a wonderful man
And it's hard for you to understand
That he won't be around anymore
God took him home a few days ago

Your days sometime seem very dark
But God will supply your needs
Always remember keep his love in your heart
He'll be there in spirit and you'll never be apart

The love you feel can make you happy
When you remember the good each day
There're times you may be up and sometimes down
When sorrow comes, you can always pray

Brothers

Three brothers born on different days Trevell, Travis, Tim-O-Thy

Even though they are miles apart
The love they have for each other will forever remain in their
hearts

Separated by the space of time
The joy of friendship the three brothers feel
Are etched in the corners of their minds

Yes! We are our brothers' keeper; the bible tells us so
If we are accountable to each other,
Our love and friendship will continue to grow.
Sometimes the rain will fall, other times the wind will blow.
We are anchored together in the spirit,
Because the word tells us so.

Three Brothers Trevell, Travis, and Tim-O-Thy
Trevell absent from the body, present with the Lord.
Oct 6, 1989 – March 10, 2012

Penned by Trevell H. Brown

"I Can Do All Things Through Christ"

The question that is asked is, "what would a college education do for me as an individual and what goals do I have?" Well, I have given it much thought and I believe that going to college would be a perfect way to not only further my education, but also guide me in choosing the career that will help me to succeed in life, both professionally and personally. I've been attending school for twelve years now, I'm 18 years old and I'm a senior at Palm Bay High School. My senior year, so far, has not been as easy as I thought, with taking SAT's and ACT's, it's been a lot of hard work. I truly believe that this year has been the year that I've matured quite a bit. It has taught me to be very responsible in my studies. Almost every week I come across a difficult task that challenges me mentally and physically, from completing homework assignments to bettering myself in sports.

In high school I have had to face many challenges, both personally and academically, and I feel that I have learned to overcome many obstacles and have learned from those obstacles. But, I honestly believe that I wouldn't be able to overcome anything without the One who made all things possible, and that's the One and Only, Jesus Christ. And I truly believe that I can do all things through Christ Jesus, who strengthens me.

My overall goal is to complete college and receive a degree that I can be proud of. With that degree, I plan to go on and become a successful mechanical engineer and design the next car of the future. However, I also know that over the next few years I may change my mind and decide that my future career path may lead me in a different direction. No matter what that direction is, I know that the path will be one that I plan to enjoy and learn and share with others along the way. When I have finished college I will look back and be able to say I enjoyed myself, made new friendships, helped others, received an outstanding education and became a better man.

Once I have completed college and I am a successful business man, I plan to take care of my mother and grandmother, financially and do my best to repay them for all of the wonderful things they have done and sacrificed for me over the years. Without their guidance and the support of my church and community and teachers I would not have made it to college.

When I look into the future, I see a man that would make people proud to be around. I will hopefully be married and a father, a leader in my community and will be giving back to students, such as myself. I will explain to them the difference that a college education can make in one's life!

Most of all I give thanks to GOD for not only giving me the opportunity to make it through high school, but a chance to go to college to be more than what I am today. And to my mother, I promise I would be more than a man, I'm going to be a strong man.

Learning From the Best To Avoid Pitfalls

Attending college would be a gigantic step for me. It's actually the first step I would have to take on my own, something I'm looking forward to. From time to time, I was constantly reminded how important it would be to be the first male out of three generations to graduate from high school, go on to college to further my education, and break what is known as the generational curse.

Throughout high school I have continued to use a bible verse that I learned at an early age – "I can do all things through Christ Jesus who strengthens me." Not only do I say this verse constantly, but I truly believe that this verse was set to give me strength and courage to continue my journey, and to be the successful man I was destined to be.

My entire life I have seen family and friends make wrong choices that have led them to be incarcerated for the majority of their life and becoming part of the world's system as it is today. For that reason, I am thankful for making the right decision, to rewrite history. I am also very grateful to God for directing my path and I know I'm up for any challenge that comes my way, because this is what I truly desire in my heart.

I really don't know my great-grandfather; he passed away at the age of 92 when I was only 10 years old. From what I do remember, he seemed like a very intelligent, strong, family man. I was told that my great-grandfather only achieved up to a 4th grade education, although, that didn't hinder him from becoming the intelligent family man that he was.

He was the father of sixteen children. He made sure that every last child had food to eat and a place to sleep, even if it meant him not eating until everyone else was fed. He raised his children to be respectful, loving and kind. He taught them to do unto others as you would have them do unto you.

I was told that my great-grandfather was an excellent father. My grandmother told me a story that she remembered very well. My great-grandfather needed a pair of shoes and so did she. He chose to get my grandmother shoes. She said she was so excited about her new pair of shoes. The next morning her happiness was crushed when she saw her father curing card board from a box to stuff his shoes and wrapping a string around it to keep his feet from touching the ground. At that moment she realized that her father would go to any length to ensure that all of their needs would be met.

For most of his life he was a farmer, until the family relocated from Jennings, Florida to Eau Gallie, Florida where things began to change. With a 4th grade education he became a veterinarian assistant for 15 years, he was also the pastor of two churches, and after retiring at the age of 65 he started a lawn service business where most of his clients were doctors and lawyers.

When I think of my great-grandfather for accomplishing so much with so little, I see myself following in his footsteps; determined to provide for my family as much as he did and I know with a higher education, the sky is the limit.

My grandmother only had a 10th grade education. She dropped out of school to be a caregiver for her mother after suffering from a heart attack. My grandmother is a strong, energetic, outgoing person. She is the mother of four and worked two jobs to take care of her family. My grandfather, whom I never met, left home in 1972 to start a new family.

I understand without a high school education, my grandmother had the best of jobs. She was the manager of Kmart apparel for 10 years and transferred to New Orleans, LA in 1983 and six years later, I was born. My grandmother hosted a radio program for six years while in New Orleans. She owned and operated her own business, called Della Domestic Service, for three years, in West Palm Beach, Florida. In 1999, when her father died she moved back to Melbourne, Florida to take care of the family business. My grandmother is now a play writer. She travels with a cast of 20 members to produce her Gospel play "Be Careful How You Entertain Strangers."

I have learned a lot from my grandmother and she has spoken a lot of wisdom into my life and she continues to encourage me to further my education in life. For the past few years I have traveled to Philadelphia to visit my aunt and uncle who have always been a source of inspiration and encouragement for my life. My uncle is a very gifted man with many talents. He has taught me a lot about life, and how to be a positive role model for my brothers who are growing up in these trying times. I have learned a lot from him. I've also learned not to settle for little, but to reach for everything. I will continue to carry his wisdom with me throughout college.

Although I wasn't born during the civil rights movement, I've learned in school that Martin Luther King Jr. was a proud black man. He paved the way for many to have the opportunity to afford a college education. His life was taken before he had the chance to run for any political office, however, his legacy lives on. For that reason, we as black people should excel because of the foundation he laid for us.

A man that is living out his dream today is Barack Obama. He faces challenges every day; from the media to opposing parties. However, he continues to focus on what he believes is right and has made a choice not to let negativity get in his way. He inspires me, knowing that nothing is impossible to achieve, only if I stay focused and reach for my highest expectations.

Just with a high school diploma is not enough to get a secure job to survive through these economic conditions. With gas prices increasing, and food prices escalating, it makes it hard for people to survive. With a college education, it will prepare me for a substantial job. So, I will be able to provide for my family despite the struggle.

I have seen many friends come short of completing high school by letting the streets consume their every emotion, without regards to other's safety. Many friends have tried to influence me to turn to the streets and do things that I know would put me behind bars and I would not have the opportunity to complete my education and for that reason, I am very grateful for the decisions that I have made.

I would like to express my gratitude to the Ricardo Ramharrack Foundation for giving me the opportunity to apply for this scholarship. I am very sorry that a life had to end for me to have the chance to further my education. However, I am grateful for this opportunity that has been bestowed upon me.

Our Precious Gift

By Dia Davis

October 6, 1989, our precious gift of God was born
He was on loan just a short time
Not knowing March 10, 2012, would not be the norm

The sudden departure of our Gift
Has left many hearts so grieved
The Lord only wants what's best for us all
And unknowingly, Trevell quickly took a leave

Surrendering his life to Jesus, at the tender age of six
One may say, "He's too young to understand"
But yet, his baptism God did permit

A determination inside him, to further his education in college
Although it meant working two full time jobs
It was worth it all, just to obtain knowledge

Hard Task? Yes it was, but you never heard him complain
For the choice was his to make
Without hard work and struggles, there can be no gain

Wisdom was another virtue that our Gift portrayed
Young and old would seek his advice, many would leave amazed

We won't forget his family, that he loved so very much
Coming to see Auntie Nauna, with a special touch

Stroking her hair expressing his love, one could truly see
She was special in his eyes, and would forever be
A very precious love for mama, Trevell
Only God and she could understand

The day she held her baby in her arms, God had a master plan
Their relationship was unique, a purpose Trevell was in her life
If nothing but to mentor others, that there is hope in sight

It's not easy my cousin, for you to endure this cross
But intercession through family and friends
Will help us with your loss

A special love for Auntie Carolyn
For she too, took him as her own
During his early childhood years, He was never alone
She loved and cared for him, and now shed many tears
For the baby she knew and helped to raise, is no longer here

His memories will linger in her heart
Of all the shared happy times
But she must release Trevell into the hands of our Saviour
And declare, "Peace Be Thine"

He found the relationship with his earthly father Fred
With no hesitation, many sons would desire
And now he's with his Heavenly Father, way up in the sky

After graduating from high school, and off to college he went
Precious Uncle Robert and Auntie Michelle
Knew from God an Angel was sent

Their love for him endless, as he called for early Morning Prayer
2 or 3 o'clock in the morning, some would only dare

Never ever forget Grandma Della, who was there from the start
Everyone knew he had a great love for her
That could only come from the heart

Being his main supporter, assuring he had no need
Working, making phone calls and don't forget the prayer
In order for Trevell to succeed

Trevell was not a fighter
Not his purpose for being here
When the taunter observed their surroundings
Big sister TaQuanda would appear

Feeling responsible for her brother, she didn't come for talk
Now there is compatibility here, let's get it on
Don't just stand and gawk

The correction toward his brothers
That obedience is better than sacrifice
He did it because he loved you so you would have a fulfilled life

Best friend Devin, you were as macaroni and cheese
Know that he had a special love for you (and mama Stacey)
Trust in God, and he will be everything you need

The young man's testimony of how Trevell impacted his life
He is not the only one, but there is hope in sight

The gift that God lent to us, has truly been a light
And now that his light has diminished
We sadly say to our precious Trevell
Good night…

God Got Me

On Thursday, March 8th, approximately 6pm, the telephone rang. As I picked up the receiver I could hear excitement in Trevell's voice. He said Gran-ma, "what have I been waiting on for some time now?" I replied, "I don't know baby, tell me about it." He said, "the job Gran-ma, the job". I was sitting here on the computer, feeling a little sad and down in my spirit because I had applied for a position some time ago. Even though I already have a job, the job at the Mental Health Center is the one I really wanted. I spoke to myself and said 10 times God Got Me, it will be alright. I pressed the button to send a message. At that very moment the phone rang. "Trevell Brown, this is Mr. Smith, I understand you are interested in the position that we have available. My secretary is very impressed with you and she informed me that you have called everyday checking on the status of the position. She wrote me a letter and placed it on my desk. She said, Mr. Smith I suggest that you hire this young man. I have never seen anyone so persistent. He will be an asset to this company. Mr. Brown, I called to offer you the position and I would like for you to start on Wednesday."

Gran-ma he said, "didn't I tell you everything would be alright. God Got Me. Oh, how was your day Gran-ma? Were you running around all day doing things for the family? You need to slow down. I am so happy about this job Gran-ma I'm going to take care of you. Okay love you Gran-ma. I'll call you tomorrow, good-bye." That was the last conversation we had.

Early Saturday morning just past midnight, Glenda and Carlton came into my room, turned on the light and sat down.   I knew something was wrong. It was hard for Carlton to speak. He said there was an accident. Trevell is gone Mama. He and Jessie died. At that moment I knew for some time that the Holy Spirit had been sending me a message. On Wednesday, the day before our last conversation I stood in the middle of my living room and spoke these words aloud, "Devil you are a liar my grandson, Trevell, will live and not die." I had seen the accident, however, I did not want to believe it.

Trevell is now living with Christ. To live is Christ and to die is gain. The Word tells us that God will give us our hearts desire. He granted Trevell the last thing he ever asked for, the position he wanted so very much. Though he did not live long enough to work the job, God allowed him to receive the job. Trevell's famous words were "I can do all things through Christ who gives me Strength"…living a full life, trusting in God to deliver on time.

He's an on time God; He may not come when you want Him to, however, He is always on time.

"God Got Me, Gran-ma, God Got Me"

Let not your heart be troubled ye believe in God believe also in me. In my father house there are many mansions, if it were nto so I would have told you. I go to prepare a place for you. And if I go and prepare a place for you I will come again and receive you unto myself, that where I am there where you may also be.

John 14:1-3 KJV

Gran-Ma's Boy

It's hard to say good-bye
To the one you love so much
I will bless the lord always
For the gentleness of your touch

It's hard to say good-bye
Because we communicated so often
I miss your voice that sound so sweet
I pray also to the Lord your soul to keep

It's hard to say good-bye
We shared so many precious moments
You will remain forever in my heart
Through the rain and the thunder
Dark clouds will roll away
The sun always brings a brighter day

It's hard to say good-bye
However you have run your race
You have kept the faith
Now that your journey has ended
You will see Jesus face to face

It's hard to say good-bye
I will meet you again some day
In the home beyond the sky

It's hard to say good-bye
Gone but not forgotten
I'll carry you in my heart
God created you special from the start

It's hard to say good-bye
But I must let you go
The dark clouds will roll away
In Christ Jesus there is a brighter day

It's hard to say good-bye
Thanks for travelling this way
Even though you didn't have long to stay
Trevell, you were the best of the best
Now you have Gran-ma's permission to take your rest

Prayer of Freedom

The Scott Family Seed

Father God in the Name of Jesus the Christ,

I come before you this day into Your Holy presence with thanksgiving, by the power of Your Holy Spirit. Lord, I thank You for Your grace and mercy. I thank You that You are a kind, loving and compassionate God that continues to watch over us daily, keeping us from all hurt, harm, and danger. I come to You this morning, while the dew is still on the rose, on behalf of the Scott Family Seeds of Pastor Johnie and Rosa Scott. Thank You for the wisdom You instilled in our parents which they imparted into our lives. They taught us good values, and how to depend on the Word of God for direction. They taught us to love the Lord our God with all our hearts, soul and mind. In the Name of Jesus, we ask that You keep us in Your will and way. We declare Your righteousness. Thank You Lord for setting us free from things that may hold us captive. Thanks that You deliver us from sin and evil, washing us whiter than snow by the blood that You shed for each of us. Help us Lord to run this race with patience that is set before us. That we may run and not be weary, walk and not faint as we look unto Jesus the Author and Finisher of our faith. We are grateful that we are overcomers by the Blood of the lamb; we walk by faith and not by sight. We thank You for miracles that have been performed in our family. We pull down miracles from the atmosphere. You said miracles, signs, and wonders will follow us. We thank You for wisdom, knowledge and understanding that You've blessed us with. Thank You for giving us an undivided heart that we may serve You, daily. Our hearts desire is to please You always. As members of the Body of Christ we choose to live

Holy in Your sight. We bless You, Lord, for giving us spiritual insight as we look into the mirror for inspection through the Word of God. We do realize that there are things we can improve on by obeying Your precepts. Help us as a family to love one another and to put away those differences that separate us from each other and disconnect us from the Holy Spirit. We are one body yet many members fitly joined together. I do know that there are many family members that are not yet saved, we lift them up to You right now laying them at the foot of the cross, and we ask, in the Name of Jesus, that You draw each of them close to Your bleeding side. Call them out of darkness that they may turn their hearts toward You. I know that You want us all saved and we are ready to do our part as You have commissioned us to do. We will continue to pray until there is a break through. In the Name of Jesus, we pull down every strong hold and we ask, in the Name of Jesus, that You restore everything that the enemy has stolen from our family. We give thanks that every tormenting spirit is destroyed. We thank you for grace to overcome generational curses. We acknowledge and confess the sins of our forefathers. We take a stand and authority over the evil one and all iniquities traced, in the mighty Name of Jesus. We apply the Blood of Jesus over our hearts, minds, souls and bodies. We rejoice and confess the blessing of the Lord for a thousand generations. We do receive all Heavenly resources that are available to us right now; help us to move in the direction that You are leading us. Thank You for a turnaround as we fulfill our potential and move forward in Jesus' Name. The effectual, fervent prayer of a righteous man availeth much…we are standing on the promises of God, that no weapon formed against us shall prosper. In the mighty Name of Jesus the Christ we present this prayer to You…

…speaking those things that are not as though they were, every stronghold broken…

Unforgiveness
Bondage
Envy
Idolatry
Fear
Doubt
Homosexuality
Drug Abuse
Guilt
Hatred
Temptation
Revenge
Immorality
Laziness
Dishonesty
Worry
Disobedience
Low Self-esteem

My Daily Prayer

*What a friend we have in Jesus. All our sins and grieves to bear…All because
we do not carry everything to God in Prayer."[i]*

We walk by faith not by sight. We are confident and would rather
be absent from the body, and present with the Lord. God is able to
make all grace abound toward you, that ye always having all
sufficiency in all things. May abound to every good work." Thank
you Lord, that your grace is sufficient for us all. My strength is
made perfect in weakness. Give us faith to trust you Lord. I am
crucified with Christ. Nevertheless, I live. Yet not I, but Christ
liveth in me and the life which I now live in the flesh, I live by
faith of the Son of God who loved me and gave Himself for me. I
desire to be present with you as I walk in the Spirit and I shall not
fulfill the lust of the flesh. Thank You for the fruit of the Spirit:
love, joy, peace, long-suffering, gentleness, goodness, faith,
meekness and temperance. If we live in the Spirit, let us also walk
in the Spirit. Help us to bear one another's burdens. Be not
deceived. God is not mocked. For whatsoever a man soweth that
shall he also reap. As we have opportunity, let us do go unto all
men, especially unto them who are of the household of faith. In
the Name of Jesus, we bless You, the God and Father of our Lord,
Jesus Christ, who hath blessed us with all spiritual blessings in
Heavenly places in Christ. We cease not to give thanks to You for
Your spiritual wisdom and revelation in knowledge. Thank you
Lord, for the eyes of our understanding that we may know the hope
of Your calling. We are alive because of Your grace and mercy,
for by grace are we saved through faith, because it is a gift from
God. Thank you Lord Jesus Christ, that You dwell in our hearts by
faith, that we may be grounded and rooted in love. There is one
Lord, one faith and one baptism. One God and Father of all, which

is above all and through all and in all. We come before You on behalf of all married couples, help them to continue in love and faithfulness. The Word of God tells us that husbands should love their wives, even as Christ also loves the church and gave himself for it. Wives continue to submit to your husbands as unto the Lord, praying always with all prayer and supplication in the Spirit, taking the helmet of salvation and the sword of the Spirit, which is the Word of God. Grace be to you and peace from God, our father and from the Lord Jesus Christ, being confident of this very thing, that He which hath begun a good work in you will perform it until the day of Jesus Christ. Be careful for nothing, but in everything, by prayer and supplication, with thanksgiving, let your request be made known unto God. And the peace of God which passeth all understanding shall keep your hearts and minds through Christ Jesus. Let your speech be always with grace, seasoned with salt, that ye may know how ye ought to answer every man. But I would not have you be ignorant brethren, concerning them which are asleep. That ye sorrow not, even as others which have not hope.*1* For if we believe that Jesus died and rose again, even so them also which sleep in Jesus, will God bring with Him. For the Lord himself shall descend from Heaven with a shout, with the voice of the archangel and with the trumpet of God and the dead in Christ shall rise first. Then we which are alive and remain shall be caught up together in the cloud to meet the Lord in the air. And so shall we ever be with the Lord. Wherefore, comfort one another with these words. *Thessalonians 4:13-18* Lord Jesus, help us to be patient toward all men. See that none render evil for evil unto any man; but even follow that which is good, both among yourselves and to all men. Rejoice, pray without ceasing. In everything give thanks for this is the will of God in Christ Jesus concerning us. We will not quench the Spirit, or despise prophesying. Help us to prove all things. Hold fast to that which is good and continue to abstain from all appearance of evil. And the very God of peace sanctify you wholly; and I pray that the body of Christ's spirit, soul and body be preserved blameless unto the coming of our Lord Jesus Christ. Greet all brethren with a holy kiss. May the Lord direct our hearts into the love of God and into the patient writing of Christ. But the Lord is faithful, who shall stablish you and keep you from evil. We thank Christ Jesus our Lord, who has enabled us for that He counted us faithful, putting us into ministry. This is a true saying, if a man desire the office of a bishop, he desireth a good work. For God hath not given us the spirit of fear, but of power, and of love, and of a sound mind. Hold fast the words which thou has heard of me, in faith and love which is in Christ Jesus. *2 Timothy 1:13* All scripture is given by inspiration of God, and is profitable for doctrine, for reproof, for correction, for instruction in righteousness. *2 Timothy 3:16* I charge thee therefore before God, and the Lord Jesus Christ. Preach the word in season and out of season. Be watchful in all things. Endure afflictions. Do the work of an evangelist. Make full proof of your ministry that being justified by His grace, we should be made being perfect according to the hope of eternal life. God, I thank You for the confidence and obedience, for we have great joy and consolation in thy love. Let us draw near with a true heart in full assurance of faith having hearts sprinkled from an evil conscience and our bodies washed with pure water. Now faith is the substance of things hoped for and the evidence of things not seen. *Hebrews 11:1* But without faith it is impossible to please God. For he that cometh to God must believe that He is a rewarder of them that diligently seek Him, looking unto Jesus, the author and finisher of our faith. Who for the joy that was set before him endured the cross. Despising the shame and is sat down at the right hand of the throne of God and make straight paths for your feet, lest that which is lame be turned out of the way; but let it rather be healed. *Hebrews 12:13* Help us to be doers of the word and not hearers only, deceiving our own selves. As we submit ourselves to you God, we resist the devil and he will flee from us. In the Name of Jesus, we thank you for clean hands. Purify our hearts. Help us to humble ourselves in the sight of the Lord and He will lift us up. It is written, "Be ye holy, for I am holy. *1 Peter 1:16* Cast all your cares upon the Lord, He cares for you. The day of the Lord will come like a thief in the night. Lord, help us to be ready when You return. Whatsoever we ask, we receive of Him, because we keep His commandments and do those things that are pleasing in His sight. May the grace of God be with us. In the Name of Jesus, In which above all things, that the body of Christ may prosper and be in good health even as our souls prospereth. Help us to keep ourselves in the love of God, looking for the mercy of our Lord Jesus Christ unto eternal life. I was in the Spirit, on the Lord's day. I thank You that You are the Alpha and Omega. You are the First and the Last. He that has an ear to hear what the Spirit of the Lord saith to the church; Lord, we thank You that our ears are open, that we may receive from You. Help us not to be lukewarm Christians, because You said that You would spew us out of Your mouth. We give thanks to our Lord and Savior Jesus Christ for blessing us with the power of Your Word, in the Name of Jesus we present this prayer to you from Your Word.

AMEN!!!

---

[i] ***"What A Friend We Have In Jesus"***...*Joseph M. Scriven, 1855*

Della Scott Thomas is an anointed vessel of God who loves to assist people that have a special need. She is a loving and caring person, who displays the love of God wherever she goes. She is the founder of D. S. T. Production, the producer of a play "Be Careful How You Entertain Strangers", and very active in the church she attends. She works with the Prayer Ministry, Outreach Ministry, and assists with other activities in the church.

Congratulations, Sis! All these years of writing your thoughts and dreams down has finally paid off. You have always been creative and very active. Sis, you are a rock in our family and we love and appreciate your wisdom and stamina that God has given you to share with others. I know that if anyone could become an author in the family, it would be you. It takes a great deal of talent, effort, and determination to achieve such a challenging goal. It's very inspiring to me to see my sister's name printed on a book. I love you very much! You have been here for me and the family so many times and I give you accolades for a job well done. This book will be my gift to some people I know.

I cannot wait to celebrate this wonderful achievement with you. I'm very proud of you. I *look forward to having you autograph your book for me. Again, congratulations, Sis! If Mom and Dad were here today, they would be proud as I am for you fulfilling one of your goals.*

M. H. Scott-Brown